To Harold Kraushar,
a man whose eyes brighten
whenever he sees a deer

Library of Congress Cataloging in Publication Data Arnosky, Jim. Deer at the brook. Summary: A poetic and pictorial portrayal of the lovely things that happen at a brook as a mother deer and two fawns come to drink, fish leap, and sunlight sparkles on the water. 1. Deer—Juvenile literature. [1. Deer. 2. Animals] I. Title. QL737.U55A76 1985 599.73'57 84-12239 ISBN 0-688-04099-3 ISBN 0-688-04100-0 (lib. bdg.)

Deer at the Brook

JIM ARNOSKY

LOTHROP, LEE & SHEPARD BOOKS
New York

The brook is a sparkling place—
sunlight on water, water on stones.

The brook is a place
deer come to.

Some come alone.

Some come together.

Mothers bring their fawns
to drink . . .

and to eat.

They walk in the water.

They watch the fish leap.

They play on the sandy bank

and nap in the sun.

Sunlight on water, water on stones —

the brook is a sparkling place.

F0